SOAP

*He wont be
happy
till he
gets it!*

SOAP

MAKING IT
ENJOYING IT
BY
ANN
BRAMSON

WP Workman Publishing Company New York

ACKNOWLEDGMENTS

Thanks to Dr. Mario Novakovic, Peter Workman, Nancy Balavich, Morton Bramson, and Dr. Frances Lewis

Illustrations by Norma Erler Rahn

Workman books are available at special discounts when purchased in bulk for premiums and sales promotions as well as for fund-raising or educational use. Special editions or book excerpts can also be created to specification. For details, contact the Special Sales Director at the address below.

Workman Publishing Company, Inc.
708 Broadway
New York, N.Y. 10003

ISBN: 0-911104-57-7
Cover photographs by Jerry Darvin
Cover design by Paul Hanson
Typeset by Trade Composition
Printed and bound by the George Banta Company
Manufactured in the United States of America

Second edition

First printing, April 1975

20   19   18   17   16   15

FOR ARTHUR

"Have You a Little Fairy in Your Home?"

Contents

Homemade Soap and the Satisfaction to Be Had in Making It

HOMEMADE SOAP has little to do with store-bought soap. Though they function similarly, homemade soap is much the better. Where the hard pastel-colored bars sold at the drugstore are anonymous and indifferent, homemade soap has character. It charms. Even Ivory, which soap enthusiasts favor for its integrity, seems ersatz in comparison to a bar of homemade soap.

Homemade soap smells good. It smells genuine, like the ingredients from which it is made. It makes the body smell like a body should. If you care to perfume your soap, to round its edges, you won't end up with a standardized odor, something that smells chemically floral or sweet.

Homemade soap feels good: soft, rich, enveloping, soothing. The lather is dense and penetrating rather than thin and airy. It leaves an emollient film on your skin that makes it feel soft and sensuous. Homemade soap is comforting in ways which manufactured soap can never be: its look, its weight, its bulk, how it feels in your hands, looks in its dish. There is something ineffable about homemade soap. It's not homogenized, pasteurized, deodorized, sanitized, synthesized—it's one of a kind, every bar is different, each unique. It is idiosyncratic in the way of all homemade and handmade things.

There is something reassuring about being able to supply yourself with a necessity. Making things for yourself fosters a more personal and reciprocal relationship between you and the objects around you. A participant in the labors, you more thoroughly enjoy the fruit of them.

Soap is fundamentally made of just two ingredients—fat and lye. Odd, two elements that possess such dubious reputations should combine to make something as noble as soap. Odd marriages, interesting offspring.

Soapmaking requires the learning of a technique or a craft skill. Your first batch may not turn out quite the way it should, but you mustn't let this discourage you. Each succeeding batch will be better because you will be able to apply knowledge learned in the doing. It can be a messy business, be forewarned. But often things worth doing involve some mess.

Before we begin to make soap ourselves it

is well to have an overall view of the processes involved. The fat and lye (which is first dissolved in water to make a lye solution) are mixed together at the temperature most favorable for initiating the soapmaking reaction, which is called saponification. It is a chemical reaction: the ingredients come in contact with one another, mingle, interact, and turn into a new product which is a combination of soap and glycerin. In manufactured soaps, most of the glycerin is removed and sold separately because of its commercial value in other industries. Homemade soap retains its natural glycerin, making it all the nicer. Glycerin is very soothing.

The reaction begins in the pot in which the fat and lye solution are combined. The mixture is stirred continuously and slowly thickens as soap begins to form. The soap is not left to harden in the pot but is poured while still liquid into boxes which serve as molds. Here saponification continues and—eventually—ends. After a day or two, the soap can be removed from the molds and either sliced into bars or left whole. It is then set aside uncovered where air can circulate about it for two or three weeks. This aging improves the soap. After aging, the soap is ready for use.

Though soap can be made from just grease and lye, the recipes that follow use combinations of fats and oils to make a richer and more sophisticated soap. These soaps are out-and-out toilet soaps. They are excellent soaps, fine to use on your skin. They are not laundry soaps. Nor are they the soaps made by our great-aunts and our grandmothers. They are better.

Ingredients and Equipment

INGREDIENTS

MOST OF the soap recipes in this book call for beef fat, more properly, for tallow, which is rendered beef fat. You can get beef fat from your butcher. (You do your own rendering.) If you explain to him why you need the fat, it may modify his initial reaction. Then again, it may not. He will look at you askance. Persevere. You *do* know what you're talking about. If you are fortunate you may find a butcher who comes from a family with a soapmaking tradition. A man with roots. He will take you under his wing, give you all the fat you want, and if you buy your meats from him, the best cuts are yours for the asking.

Most often there will be no charge for the fat. Sometimes you will be charged ten cents a pound. More than twenty cents a pound and you're dealing with a crook.

Some will say, "Fat? You don't want fat, you want suet." Suet is fat from around the kidney area. There are prime meats and there are prime fats. Suet is a prime fat. However, as there is a good deal more fat around the muscles, I would not suggest waiting until you accumulate enough suet to commence soapmaking. If it is offered, there is no reason not to accept, unless the price is steep. Both suet and muscle fat can be used together. Suet feels less oily; it is a richer, more solid, drier fat. Unlike other muscle fat, it can be crumpled and broken up into pieces by hand. It may be more pleasant to use, but beef fat is beef fat, one will never feel terribly attached to it whether it comes from one part of the steer's body or another.

Try to get your butcher to cut off as much meat and extraneous matter as possible. At the risk of being accused of lunacy you could take your request one step further and ask your butcher to put the fat through his meat grinder. Ground to the consistency of ground chuck the fat will render twice as fast. One butcher offered to do this for me. Another balked. Having the fat ground is not necessary.

One of the recipes calls for lard. Lard is certainly simple to use. It takes no processing. You buy it at the supermarket and just throw it in the pot. For those who don't want to use animal fats at all, there is a Vegetable Soap which is made with Crisco (or any other hydrogenated shortening), olive oil, and coconut oil. Olive oil and shortening are always available at the supermarket. Coconut oil, however, is a little hard to get a hold of. Do not buy it at drugstores, as they will charge you a fortune. Try to get it from some other source. At different times I have bought coconut oil from vegetable oil wholesalers, Hispanic food stores, chemical supply houses, health food stores, and pharmacies. That's in order of increasing expense—least expensive was the oil wholesaler; most expensive, the pharmacies. I haven't tried bakery suppliers—coconut oil is often used by bakeries.

You'll have to do some searching to find a wholesaler and, if you find one, some pretty fast talking to get them to sell you anything less than a fifty-ton barrel. (What you want is a gallon; the cost should be about five dollars.) Look through the classified phone directory under Oils, Vegetable and under Coconut Oil.

The Spanish and Puerto Rican food stores, the chemical supply houses, and the health food stores usually sell pint bottles, weighing about a pound, which is a little short of what you'll need. You'll have to get two.

Recently I came upon a perfectly wonderful source, a place called Walnut Acres. It is one of the oldest and finest organic farms in this country and is run by some very special people. They mail-order their products all over the country and can send you coconut oil in quart and gallon tins at prices that almost rival the wholesalers. They are running about two and a half dollars for a quart and seven and a half for a gallon, not including postage. It's best to write first and check, as their prices fluctuate with availability. (At Walnut Acres, prices are even known to go down.) Ask for their catalogue (Walnut Acres, Penns Creek, Pennsylvania 17862). A quart is plenty for any recipe, and a gallon more economical if you think you'll be making a few batches. The oil stores well.

Coconut oil is expressed from the coconut. It is liquid to semisolid at room temperature; heated slightly it turns liquid; refrigerated it becomes quite brittle. It need not be refrigerated, though your beef fat and lard should be.

Castor oil is used in one recipe and is easily obtained from a drugstore.

Lye is a constant ingredient in all soaps but in pure or concentrated form it can be dangerous. It's available in most supermarkets and hardware stores among the cleaning supplies. Red Hook, Indco, and B. T. Babbit's are three common brands; there are others. Don't get Lysol or other lye concoctions. You want pure lye. It comes in thirteen ounce containers which are usually red, white, and blue. The net weight indicated on the container is never accurate, so don't use it as a gauge in measuring.

Lye is also referred to as caustic soda. These terms are used interchangeably. Technically, lye is a term describing a group of chemicals. Its proper name is caustic soda. When we refer to something as being too caustic, we mean it contains too much free lye.

Lye was originally made by running water through wood or plant ashes. When all soap was homemade in this country, rural folks made their own lye, "leached" their own lye is how the phrase goes. Homemade lye produces a soft or liquid soap due to the fact that the lye leached from wood is a potassium lye or caustic potash. Hard soaps are made with a sodium lye or caustic soda.

Legend has it that lye's soapmaking proclivity was come upon accidentally in ancient times. On a mountaintop there was a pagan temple where animals were sacrificed to the gods. The wood ashes from the fire and the melted animal fats ran down the slope of the mountain to the banks of a river. Women who washed their clothes on the banks found that when the river was yellowed with altar drippings their laundry came cleaner.

Lye is now made from a common salt solution. The salt is electrolytically transformed into lye.

There is little I can say in defense of lye. It is not a well-liked substance, and learning to love it would require a leap of faith. The lye companies recommend using it to open clogged drains and in the preparation of pretzels and hominy; also to remove fruit skins, peel beets, and cure olives. A motley selection of possibilities, no? I do not understand lye, but so be it. It is essential to soapmaking, and if used with care should create no problem at all.

Lye is inert in its dry form; however, it attracts water. If you get a flake on you and it sits there unnoticed, perspiration or moisture in the air may eventually activate it and cause a severe burn. This has happened to me only once in all my soapmaking days, working barefoot and carelessly spilling lye about as though it were confetti. It is worth avoiding. Lye in solution, though less dangerous, also requires caution in handling. Though precautions are taken, you may come in contact with it accidentally. This is not catastrophic—the solution burns, stings, maybe itches. Run the abused member under cold water or rinse with vinegar or lemon juice to relieve the burn.

Do keep lye far away and out of the hands of children, as it can be fatal when swallowed. And be particularly careful about your eyes. As you yourself are not likely to swallow lye or to bathe in it, there is little real cause for fear. Regardless, it is a good idea to familiarize yourself with the cautions detailed on the lye container label.

All the soaps in this book are made from

some combination of the foregoing ingredients. They combine to make the highest quality toilet soap. To make fancy soaps—scented or textured or superfatted or what have you—the addition of other ingredients may be necessary. They are mentioned when they come up in our discussion.

EQUIPMENT

ALL INGREDIENTS must be weighed out —the lye, the water that is added to it to make a solution, the animal fats, and the oils. It is necessary to have a scale. I use a dial scale with a spring platform; other styles might be adequate, too. Get a scale that has clearly delineated half ounces. If you enjoy cooking you will find a scale a good investment. No longer need you estimate six ounces of bacon or three pounds of potatoes—you can weigh them out.

The lye solution is best prepared in a forty-ounce bottle. A bottle this size is not hard to find. Mott's Apple Juice comes in a forty-ounce bottle, as do other brands and other juices should apple not be a favorite. This bottle will be subjected to high temperatures and rapid temperature changes. I have never had a bottle crack or shatter in all my soapmaking experiments. In fact, the fruit and vegetable juices are sterilized in these same bottles at temperatures higher than we'll ever go. Nonetheless, be alerted to the remote possibility and make sure the bottle you use is rugged and without cracks or imperfections. People who live in high altitudes where the boiling point is lower might consider making the lye solution in a sturdier container—say, an old enameled coffee pot. Once the lye solution has cooled, transfer it to the glass bottle. Keep an eye on the lid to the bottle, as you will need it.

You need a pot in which to make the soap. It has to be made of enamel or stainless steel and should hold at least eight quarts. The smaller the diameter of the pot the better. Better its volume should go to its height rather than its width so you get more action out of every stir. I happen to have an enormously wide, old twelve-quart enamel spaghetti pot which I use, though it doesn't meet this last specification. Perhaps you have one, too. Don't buy a pot if you have one that will do.

Remember that throughout your soap-making venture such materials as tin, aluminum, iron, and teflon should be avoided, as lye corrodes them. Wood can be used in addition to enamel, glass, and stainless steel. A spoon made of any of these materials will be needed for stirring. You will be doing a lot of that.

The lye will discolor wooden utensils, darken them somewhat. If you are working on a butcher board counter-top, cover it with a sheet of plastic or newspaper. Protect your floors, too, whether they be wood or linoleum.

The pots and spoons recruited for soapmaking can continue to be used for cooking. The process doesn't harm them at all. Wash them well.

You need thermometers to check on the temperatures of the lye solution and the fats. You can manage with one, but it's a lot easier with two. Your thermometer should be well calibrated—with five degree graduations or less—and it has to go down as low as 90 degrees. Some meat thermometers are perfect; dairy thermometers are fine too. You could also make do with some bathtub and indoor–outdoor thermometers. Candy thermometers shouldn't be used; they don't go below 100 degrees. Don't use medicine chest thermometers; they are too finely graduated, don't register high enough and have to be shaken down.

I use two Tel-Tru Meat Thermometers which register in 5 degree increments from 50 to 270 degrees. They're sold throughout the country in hardware and houseware stores. Bloomingdale's in New York carries them, as does Bullock's in Los Angeles. The Tel-Tru thermometers come in two lengths, one with a three-inch stem, the other five inch. I use the longer of the two.

When you mix the lye and water, you

cause a reaction to take place that gives off a lot of heat—almost 200 degrees of it. If your thermometer doesn't register temperatures that high, keep it far away from the lye solution until the solution has sat overnight and cooled off. You'll ruin any thermometer you expose to temperatures it can't contain.

Your thermometers should be made of glass or stainless steel.

Rubber gloves will keep lye away from your skin. As lye does burn on contact, they are undoubtedly a good idea. I personally find them restrictive and do my best not to use them, preferring the occasional consequences. Wear an apron or work clothes, as lye can burn holes in cloth.

You will need molds for your soap. These can be shoe boxes, gift boxes, milk containers, almost anything. You can construct your own boxes out of cardboard. To make boxes functional molds, they should be lined with plastic wrap. Use plastic garbage bags. Their strength and thickness make them preferable to thin plastic wrap. Once the soap is in the molds, they must be covered to keep the soap warm. Cardboard or something flat can be used with a blanket or two on top. Styrofoam is an especially good insulator—if you come across any in your travels, put it aside for this use.

Preliminaries

RENDERING BEEF FAT

I F YOU MAKE one of the soaps with a tallow base, you will have to render the beef fat.

Rendering is more or less the process of melting or extracting (a liquid from a solid) by heat. You could render the fat on the same day as you make your soap, but as the soapmaking may take a good three hours, I would recommend seeing to this earlier. Here's how it is done.

Rendered fat, as we have said, is called tallow. Not all of the fat will render; some solid pieces will remain in the pot and are to be discarded. That which doesn't render is called cracklings.

Taking into consideration the cracklings, figure on ending up with half the amount of fat you began with. So to determine how much fat is to be rendered, double the number of ounces of tallow called for in the recipe and round that figure off to the next pound. As tallow stores well in the refrigerator and costs little, overestimating is not a hardship. Any excess can be used in your next batch, or mixed with an equal amount of butter, plus flour and water, to make an exceptionally good pie crust, particularly for pecan pies. You might also try some on a bird-feeder. Grackles and starlings like beef fat.

If after your first batch you feel soapmaking is going to become a part of your life, you should render fifteen to twenty pounds of beef fat at a time to have it on hand.

First thing to do with the fat is to cut it up into chunks—the smaller they are, the faster they will render. Stew size is fine. If you feel inspired, you can eliminate extraneous nodes, glands, and other matter that inhabit your fat.

In your big soapmaking pot, or any pot at this point, add a few inches of water. For those who prefer measurements, let's say a quart of water. Then add two tablespoons of salt. You could render over heat alone, without the water and salt, but these latter prevent the fat from darkening (which is better for your soap) and cause the impurities— dirt, meat, odd proteins—to fall to the bottom. You get the purest, cleanest fat possible.

Set the pot with salted water on a high flame. Throw in the fat as you cut it up. Cover the pot but leave the cover slightly askew, and bring to a boil. If you can't get all the fat in the pot, wait a while; as the fat renders more space will become available. When the fat begins to rise to the surface (you will see the oily swirls that announce its presence), lower the flame to a slow boil. This shouldn't take more than fifteen minutes.

The fat will take its time rendering. It doesn't need much attention. Keep the flame low so you don't burn it. Swirl things about every so often. Crunch up some fat chunks; break open a few others to expose their insides. This will speed up rendering.

After four hours you should have a good amount of fat rendered. You can continue further, but as patience is undoubtedly waning, you may end the process here. Strain off the liquid into a big bowl or pot (of any

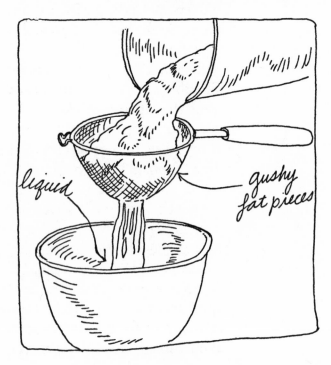

liquid

gushy fat pieces

material) and discard the gushy fat pieces. If you care to, you can squeeze out additional fat from the remaining pieces by pressing them in a potato masher. It's messy—in fact, revolting—but economical. Either way, throw all that doesn't end up in your bowl into the garbage.

Let the bowl of fat cool to room temperature, then cover it with plastic wrap or wax paper and refrigerate.

By the next day three layers will have formed: solidified tallow on top, water on the bottom, and an intermediary layer that is grey and granular. Dislodge the fat, scrape off the intermediary layer, and pour out the water. The water will probably be thick due to meat proteins. If it has jelled completely, just scrape it off and discard it. You should be left with a fine clean solid disk of tallow.

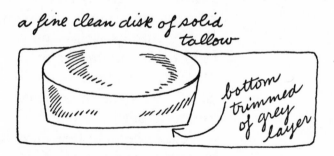

a fine clean disk of solid tallow

bottom trimmed of grey layer

Wrap it up and return it to the refrigerator until ready to use. The fat should keep in the refrigerator for two months; in the freezer it should keep indefinitely if wrapped well and not thawed and then refrozen. Should it grow rancid, you will recognize this by the smell and know to throw it out. When you are ready to make soap, the solidified tallow is weighed into the pot with the oils. It is melted once more, but it melts in a fraction of the time it took to render.

WEIGHTS AND MEASURES

ANOTHER AREA worth going over before you find yourself in its grip is how to weigh things. Time can be saved if you note the following method.

Each ingredient used in soapmaking has to be weighed out carefully. Accurate measurements are very important. To measure ingredients with a minimum of busywork, weigh them one after the other into the container in which they will end up. This is called weighing by addition. You begin by placing your big soapmaking pot on the scale. Note its weight on a piece of paper. Add to that figure the number of ounces of the first ingredient called for in the recipe. Slowly pour the ingredient into the pot on the scale until the dial reads the combined weight of pot and first ingredient. Move on to your second ingredient. Determine where the dial should rest when you have added the requisite number of ounces, and then add until you reach that point. Add all of your ingredients in this manner.

Add until dial reads the weight of the pot plus oil or fat

If you add them slowly, you will not find yourself spooning out clumps of coconut oil or teaspoons of olive oil. Start adding tallow in chunks, working your way to slivers as you get closer and closer to the exact amount you want. If you buy coconut oil in a narrow-mouthed tin or jar, you may have to melt the coconut oil to get it out. Stick the

jar in a pot of hot water and it will melt in
no time. Whether you weigh it out in liquid
or semisolid form makes no difference.

THE LYE
SOLUTION

THE LYE SOLUTION is made by adding
water to lye. Place the empty forty-
ounce bottle on the scale and slowly pour in
the number of ounces of lye called for in the
recipe. (Note the weight of the bottle, then

pour in the lye until the dial reads the combined weight of bottle plus lye.) Slowly add the water in the same manner to make the solution.

Add lye until dial reads the combined weight of bottle plus lye

Note that we are *weighing* the water: we do not want thirty-two fluid ounces (four cups of water), but thirty-two ounces by weight, which is slightly different and more precise. All measurements are avoirdupois, sixteen ounces to the pound.

OUNCES	POUNDS
2	1/8
4	1/4
8	1/2
12	3/4
16	1
24	$1^{1/2}$
32	2
40	$2^{1/2}$
48	3
56	$3^{1/2}$
64	4
72	$4^{1/2}$
80	5
88	$5^{1/2}$
96	6
104	$6^{1/2}$
112	7
120	$7^{1/2}$
128	8
136	$8^{1/2}$
144	9
152	$9^{1/2}$
160	10

Once the solution is made, remove the bottle from the scale; be careful, it is hot—almost 200 degrees. When mixed together, water and lye produce heat. It will have to cool before it can be used. Rather than wait around on soapmaking day for the temperature to drop, make your lye solution beforehand—the night before or a day or two before—and let it sit and slowly cool to room temperature. To make soap, the lye and fat are mixed when they are both between 95 and 98 degrees. It takes much less time to bring the lye up from room temperature (about 79 degrees) than to bring it down from 200 degrees.

The solution should be stirred to dissolve the lye that settles to the bottom of the bottle. Give it a stir with whatever end of a wooden spoon you can get past the mouth of

stir with a wooden spoon handle

(don't wait too long!)

the bottle. Avert your face, as the fumes are unpleasant. If you let the solution stand unmixed too long, the lye will harden and it will take some mashing and patient stirring to get it off the bottom and into solution. I have often waited too long—it is no great problem but worth avoiding as long as you have the choice. Rinse the spoon when you are through.

The lye solution is to be poured from this bottle into the soapmaking pot—it is not to be dumped in. It should be poured in a slow even stream. To effect this, simply make two holes on the top on the bottle lid with a blunt object (one on either side, as you would when opening a can). Use what-

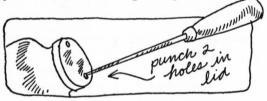

punch 2 holes in lid

ever is on hand: kitchen scissors, a screwdriver, poultry shears, skewers. Test the cap. Fill the bottle with water and see what kind of a stream you get. You want a steady

test the stream

stream of liquid, somewhat narrower than the size of a pencil or drinking straw. If you find water trickling out from under the cap and down your arm, the cap has been bent. Bend it back into shape so you have a tight seal. At all costs you want to avoid having lye trickle down your arm. See to the cap before you make the lye solution.

MOLDS

LAST THAT need seeing to are your molds. They should be prepared beforehand, as you will have no time for them once you begin making soap. Have them ready before you mix the fats and lye.

A batch of soap using any of the recipes in this book will fill one shoe box and a small gift box. A box somewhat narrower than a shoe box makes the best mold (height is to be preferred to width), but as a novice soaper, use what you have on hand. Later, when you have definite ideas about what sizes and shapes you find pleasing, and how it all looks, you can try different receptacles. Ideas for molds are discussed later in the text. If you have any small glass or ceramic ramekins—a custard dish or tiny soufflé mold—keep them in sight in case you have a little soap left over. You will not be able to remove the soap from this mold, but you can keep it near the kitchen or bathroom sink and dab at it when needed.

Cut open the sides of a plastic garbage bag so you have a flat piece, and fit it inside the boxes and up the sides. Smooth out the excess as best you can, as you don't want the plastic weaving in and out of your soap. Get it to adhere to the sides of the box. A few staples around the top of the box keeps plastic in place and lessens the interference of the excess plastic that accumulates around the corners. Gather together whatever you are going to use to cover the molds, and you are, at last, ready to begin.

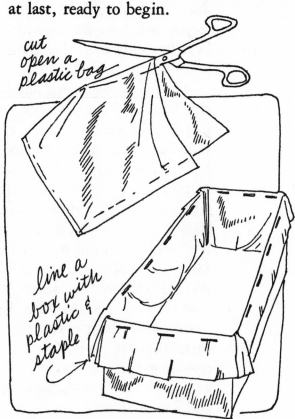

cut open a plastic bag

line a box with plastic & staple

The Recipes

HERE ARE RECIPES for four different soaps. I will not recommend one over the other, as they all should be experienced. Choose whichever appeals. All leave you clean and fresh smelling, and when shaped into bars are simply exquisite.

The first two soaps carve better because they are harder. You can do finer detail work, and get sharply defined edges and indentations. They are whiter and more responsive to coloring. The other two are milder, and because they are on the soft side, they can be shaped into balls and other forms. Should you be interested in embellishments—perhaps an Almond-Cold Cream Soap, a Butter Soap or a Superfatted Olive Oil Soap—these, too, are possible. Instructions follow the basic recipes and directions.

CASTILE SOAP

CASTILE SOAP was so-named because it was made in the Castilla region of Spain, where olives grew and good olive oil was abundant. Castile Soap has come to be known as a soap made of olive oil with tallow. A certain prestige and respect attach to it. Unfortunately it is rarely made any longer. Though soaps continue to be made in Spain, other oils are used instead of olive because of its price.

This is a hard white soap—very stately. It has fewer ingredients than the others and is the least expensive to make, as most of its weight is tallow. If you haven't been able to track down coconut oil, your problem is solved here. This soap doesn't develop a high lather, but is quite creamy and removes just as much dirt as any other.

Cut Castile into bars once it has hardened. Left as one massive piece it may become brittle and won't slice as smoothly as the others.

26 ounces olive oil
60 ounces tallow

---

11 ounces lye
32 ounces water

COPRA-OLIVE OIL SOAP

THIS IS A BEAUTY — a creamy responsive soap. The lather is exceptionally rich and nourishing. It is fast-foaming and produces large bubbles. The coconut oil is what enhances the foam. Most soaps on the market today are made of coconut oil and tallow—this one also has olive oil in it, and more's the pity manufactured soaps aren't made with olive oil, too. It is a little softer than the Castile Soap. It's color is like cream.

24 ounces olive oil
24 ounces coconut oil
38 ounces tallow

---

12 ounces lye
32 ounces water

PALMA-CHRISTI SOAP

THIS IS a very mild soap, and dry skins should respond to it favorably. It is ochre, pale yellow, very earthy. It is a little softer than the Copra-Olive Soap. Its lather is as rich but not as voluminous; the bubbles are small and thick.

Prolonged standing may bring out a bacony smell, which some may find slightly unpleasant. If you plan to have it around for a while, you might want to perfume this soap, or add a few drops of Vitamin E to your fats prior to saponification—both will check the fatty odor.

9 ounces castor oil
22 ounces olive oil
22 ounces coconut oil
32 ounces lard

11½ ounces lye
32 ounces water

**VEGETABLE
SOAP**

PRESSED TO DECIDE, I would say this soap is the mildest of them all. It has more oils, and the oils make it smoothing. It looks like the Palma-Christi Soap, soft and ochre in color. And like the Palma-Christi, the project of rendering beef fat is eliminated. Vegetarians and people who prefer not to use meat products ought to be particularly pleased with it.

> 44 ounces olive oil
> 17 ounces coconut oil
> 24 ounces Crisco or any other
>   vegetable shortening

> 10¾ ounces lye
> 32 ounces water

Making Soap

WEIGH OUT all the fats and oils into the soapmaking pot.

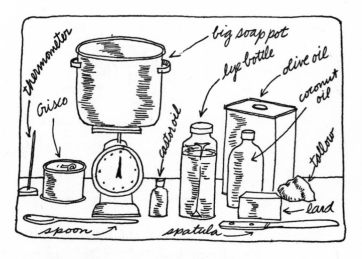

Stir the cool lye solution with the end of a wooden spoon, then rest the thermometer in the bottle.

Place the pot on a low flame and heat as slowly as possible so the temperature doesn't get too high. When three-fourths of the solid fats have melted, turn off the flame and remove the pot from the hot burner. The temperature in the pot is hot enough to melt what remains. Stir it occasionally to encourage melting.

You will now have to get the tempera-

tures of both fats and lye to between 95 and
98 degrees Fahrenheit at the same time. The
lye solution will be at room temperature,
which is around 79 degrees; the fats, if you
melted them over the lowest of flames,
should be no higher than 125 degrees.

When all the fats are melted, fill a sink or
basin with cold water and rest the soapmaking pot in it. With the second thermometer,
keep an eye on the temperature as it drops.
Don't rest the thermometer on the bottom of
the pot—immerse it in the fats to take an
accurate reading.

In about fifteen minutes, when the fats
read around 105 degrees, fill a second sink,
or basin or pot with hot water. Place the lye
solution bottle in the hot water. The lye
solution will heat up quickly—in ten,
twelve minutes. Get someone to give you a
hand—one person can watch the lye solu-

tion, while the other keeps an eye on the fats.

You shouldn't have any trouble getting the temperatures to about the same point at the same time. The knack is quickly acquired. If the fats are ready and the lye solution is not, remove the first from the water bath and let it stand until the lye reaches its range. If the lye is ready and the fats are not, let the lye rise another degree or two, remove it from the water bath, and let it stand. Should the fats fall too low, heat them up in a hot water bath. I don't recommend heating them on the stove; the temperature can be too easily knocked back up into a high range.

(Occasionally the coconut begins to solidify at 98 degrees. Do not let this worry you. Just stir it.)

You are ready to make soap when the lye solution and fats are between 95 and 98 degrees. No lower than 95, no higher than 98.

Cap your lye bottle and have it at hand. Start stirring the fats with the wooden spoon. The fats should be in motion before you add any lye, and should be kept in motion until you pour the soap into the molds. Rest the lid of the lye bottle against the rim of the pot to support some of its weight and begin introducing the lye. It should pour in a steady, even stream through one of the holes in the punctured bottle cap. Stir. Stir with a healthy vigor. If you keep the contents of the pot in motion, the lye will contact and react with as much oily matter as possible. If the elements are not well incorporated, they will separate in hardening.

rest bottle on edge of pot

As you pour in the lye, the fats, which were translucent and yellow, will turn opaque and brownish. Keep stirring. Gradually the color will become paler, a whitish yellow. (The white is soap.) These changes are not dramatic; they are subtle and hard to discern on first attempt. Patience. Stick with it. Keep stirring with an even circular movement. Don't beat it. Every so often pass through the center of the pot with your spoon, as that area is usually bypassed while stirring. Don't scrape off anything that adheres to the sides of the pot.

The mixture is ready to pour when it has the consistency of a thick pea soup, and when dripped from a spoon, traces across the surface or leaves a trail. If the drops just drop in

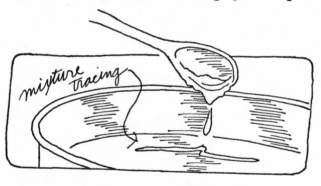

and disappear, if they don't remain momentarily in relief, if you can't draw a star or line or whatever and clearly see a trace of it on the surface of the soap, it has not thickened sufficiently. Keep stirring. Or rest for three to five minutes and then go back to it. It may take from thirty minutes to an hour and a half for your soap to thicken to the proper consistency. It depends on which recipe you have tried, how accurate your temperatures were, how well you have stirred the ingredients.

When you feel the mixture is thick enough, or if you feel you can stir no longer, pour it into the molds. The molds should be covered as soon as they are filled. The reaction produces heat, which we don't want to lose abruptly. I use a collapsed corrugated cardboard box on top of the molds and then place a blanket or two over that. Styrofoam, as mentioned earlier, is an excellent insulator; use it if you should have any.

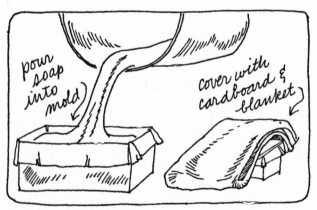

pour soap into mold

cover with cardboard & blanket

Let the soap rest. Try not to peak more than once. The soap will be hardening, will look nice and fresh, either the color of cream or white chocolate or cheese. It will look good enough to eat.

You can remove the soap from the molds twenty-four hours later. To remove, just pull from either side of the plastic. It will come out easily—no need to tear apart the box, which you might want to use for your next batch. Peel the plastic off and voilà— soap at last! And the biggest bar of soap you have ever seen. It may still be quite soft: a finger pressed on it may leave an impression. So don't drop it on the floor or handle it too much. You shouldn't really use it yet. Let it sit, uncovered, so air can circulate about it, for as long as you can resist the temptation—two weeks would be adequate, three to four even better. While your soap is aging the reaction continues to go on, though it has slowed considerably. The reaction stops when the soap has lost all the water it will. Aging gives the soap a chance to incorporate any free caustic that might be left in your soap. It improves the quality of your bar. Do give your soap this last bit of time to come into its own; your soap will be raw if it is not sufficiently cured.

You will notice there is a powdery layer on top or even about the entire block of soap. This is called soda ash. It is sodium carbonate that forms whenever caustic soda is exposed to air, and will form about your soap as it is hardening. The soda ash should be removed because it can be drying to your skin. You needn't do anything about it while your soap is aging, but you should once it is ready to use. Slice it off, as simple as that.

You can square off the edges of your soap and leave it as a block to slice off a bar whenever needed. Or you can slice the block into bars and do all sorts of elaborate things with them. (Decorative ideas are gone into later in the text.) The soap is yours to enjoy. Well earned.

Some Considerations, Problems, and Possibilities

SEPARATION AND CURDLING

IF YOUR SOAP MIXTURE separates — if the fats (which are lighter than water) rise to the top of your soapmaking pot and the lye solution falls to the bottom—it means no reaction is going on in your pot. To get your soap going again, heat the mixture to between 130 and 145 degrees, remove from the heat source, and stir. Keep stirring. The mixture should slowly turn opaque as soap begins to form. It may take a while before it thickens, as the temperature has to come down.

Should the fats and lye still refuse to combine, heat them up again (this time to the height of the temperature limit—145 degrees), and try again.

If your soap mixture curdles, take consolation in the fact that you're now a step ahead of one that's separated. In a curdled mixture you do have soap, an emulsion has formed, although it has formed improperly. In separation, if it is extreme, you haven't yet made soap. Unfortunately, a curdled mixture is also a step backward, as it's really very hard to reclaim. I'd say throw it out. If that's too distressing a proposition, play with it for a while and try your luck. Add a little more fat and/or water, heat it up, stir, but don't expect too much.

A number of things may be the cause of curdling or separation: inaccurate weights—too much or too little caustic; inaccurate temperatures; too fast or too slow addition of the lye solution—generally too fast; too rapid stirring.

Curdling and separation are sad facts. They shouldn t happen and usually don't; but sometimes they do.

MIXTURE DOES NOT THICKEN

IF YOUR MIXTURE shows no sign of thickening after an hour and a half of stirring, if it's still oily and thin, you can assume the mixture has suffered a temperature drop that has inhibited the reaction. You should be able to reactivate it by heating it up to between 120 and 130 degrees. Remove from the heat source. Stir, and stir some more.

MIXTURE DOES NOT TRACE

YOUR SOAP should trace before you pour it into the molds. That is to say, it should be thick enough to momentarily support the weight of a few drops trailed across its surface. (Tracing is discussed in full a few pages back.)

You will have no trouble getting your Castile and Copra-Olive soaps to trace. Occasionally, though, the Palma-Christi and Vegetable soaps can be a little reticent. An hour and a half of stirring is quite enough time to put into either of them. If the mixture looks thick and good, pour it into the molds even though it has not traced. However, this time, cover it better than you normally would, with three blankets or two, instead of one.

If you care to, you can take the precaution of conducting a little test. Take a whiskey jigger (a shot glass) and wash it under hot water to get it warm. Dry the glass thoroughly and spoon a sample of your soap mixture into it—about an inch deep. Let this sample sit for about ten minutes while you continue to stir your soap in the pot. If after ten minutes the soap looks fine, if there's no separation evident in the glass, you are thoroughly safe. Proceed to pour the soap into the molds.

Should there be some separation—which is most unlikely—you'll have to do some fixing. Follow the directions under Separation and Curdling. Repeat the jigger test and pour when your sample stays in the emulsion.

**BAD
BATCHES**

A SUCCESSFUL BATCH of soap does not form in layers. Severe layering is usually an indication of a mixture that has separated in the molds; one half of the soap has excessive lye, the other half has fats that haven't been saponified. One half will appear brittle and the other oily.

Except for a thin coating of soda ash on the surface, your soap should look pretty much the same throughout. The softer soaps, like the Palma-Christi and Vegetable, may look translucent around the edges. Layering may be due to insufficient stirring, too quick a temperature drop in the molds, or incorrect measurement of the lye.

Should your soap suffer just a slight separation, this can be easily remedied. The separation will be evidenced by a quarter-inch layer—on the bottom, top or sides—which is whiter, harder or shinier, in some way different from the rest. It takes a sort of soap consciousness to recognize it, but you should have that in time. Slice off the layer, and your soap is as good as new. The reason for getting rid of it is that it may be slightly drying to the skin.

A good batch of soap does not have "air bubbles" in it. In fact, these bubbles do not contain air, but are pockets of lye. If liquid drips from these pockets and if the liquid stings, you can be assured that they contain lye; and without giving it a second thought, throw the batch away. Lye pockets are due to the same factors as layering.

A good batch of soap solidifies. Should a batch remain mushy or semiliquid, something is off. If a liquid layer remains on top, you have your standard separation—this soap will not be good to use.

Be exact in your measurements and temperatures, stir continuously, quickly cover the molds once they are filled, and you should have no problems.

Do not be timid with your soap. There is no reason to be afraid of it; it won't harm you. Trust your judgment.

RECIPE ADJUSTMENTS

IF YOU ARE SHORT of one oil or fat and have a little more of another it is all right to make a few changes in the recipe as long as you don't reduce or increase the total number of ounces of fats and oils. You can use a few more ounces of one fatty ingredient if you use the same number less of another.

Other edible oils, such as cottonseed (Wesson oil is primarily soy bean and cottonseed), corn oil (Mazola), soy bean, and peanut oil, can be used in these recipes but only in small quantities. They can be used individually or mixed together. None of them encourage foaming and some leave a slight residual odor characteristic of the oil itself.

I would not recommend increasing the amount of coconut oil in any of the recipes. Coconut oil does wonderful things for soap foam, but it is drying. The other oils in the recipes counter that effect. Palm oil (not palm kernel oil) is excellent in soaps. You can use it to replace some or all of the coconut oil or part of another oil in any recipe.

In the back of the book there is a table of some oils and fats and the characteristics of soaps made with them. It will give you some idea of the qualities of different oils in soap. Should you be interested in creating your own soap recipe, I must warn you that oils have different saponification requirements. Recipes other than those that appear in this book may require different weights and temperatures.

LARGER AND SMALLER BATCHES

IF YOU WANT to make more soap at any given time, just double or triple all the ingredients in the recipe. You should have no problem. However, this is not the case should you halve or quarter a recipe. The smaller the batch, the more problems you'll have. Don't make batches smaller than the ones prescribed.

BAKED SOAP   IF YOU WANT to harden the softer soaps, bake them in the oven. Cut the soap into bars or cakes, put them on a noncorrodible baking tin or pan, and heat in a 120- to 130-degree oven for six to eight hours. This will remove the water that contributes to the soap's softness.

all starts with the scale

Digressions

IT SEEMS the history of soap and soap use is not a subject that has intrigued historians. Tomes there are on toilet bowls, but nothing on soap. Certainly this is unfair treatment of one of man's more gracious inventions, one that asks so little but gives so much.

It seems that something like soap was known as long ago as 2300 B.C. by the early civilizations of the Fertile Crescent. However, it was not necessarily used to wash with, but rather to dress one's hair or apply as a medicament to wounds. The discovery of soap and the discovery of its washing properties were by no means simultaneous.

Cleopatra, whose bath is well known, used essential oils in the rite, but no soap. The cleansing agent was a fine white sand and she came clean by abrasion.

For all the splendor of the baths of ancient Rome—with their many and varied courses of ablution—and for all their unguents, cosmetics, essences, and oils—there was no soap. An implement called the strigil was used to scrape off the oils from anointed bodies, and along with the oils, one removed some dirt.

The Romans, in time, did come to know

about soap, but its use was not widespread. Other civilizations to recognize its value were the Arabs in the Arabian Desert and then the Turks, who conquered them. The Turks probably introduced soap to Europe when they invaded the Byzantine Empire. There had always been enclaves of soapers— isolated tribes that had discovered soap, in some form or another, independently. The Vikings made it, so did the Celts. The Celts called soap *saipo,* from which our modern-day word is derived. (In Italian it is *sapone,* in Hungarian *szappan,* in Turkish *sabun, in* Spanish *jabón,* in Dutch *sepo,* in French *savon.*) The Celts were probably responsible for introducing soap to Britain, where it began to appear in the literature, under various spellings, around A.D. 1000. In 1193 there was some mention of certain soapmakers in Bristol and the unpleasant smells they created.

On the whole, however, it is not until the thirteenth century that we begin to know something more concrete of soap's history. Marseilles appears to have emerged about then as the first great center of soapmaking and remained an important producer throughout the Middle Ages. Genoa, Venice, and Bari in Italy came to rival it, as did Castilla in Spain. Like Marseilles, all had a plentiful supply of olive oil and barilla (a fleshy plant whose ashes were used to make lye). This "modern" formulation became standard for the next four to five centuries.

In the "soap-boiling" guilds and trade associations that came into existence with the rise of a merchant class or bourgeoisie, the training and advancement of workers was highly regulated, and it was only after years of proven devotion that an apprentice became a journeyman and a journeyman a master. Secrets were kept within the trade; acquired at such cost, they were not blithely relinquished. So it is to this day that much about soapmaking remains a secret and soapers remain a close-knit bunch.

Though a fair amount of soap was being made, the degree to which it was commonly used was slight. And when it was used, it was most often for laundering. Some say England's Henry IV instituted the Order of the Bath, in 1399, to prevail upon his noblemen to venture into a water-filled tub at least once in their lives—during the ritual of knighthood. Queen Isabella of Spain boasted about having had only two baths in her life, one when she was born and one when she married. Queen Elizabeth is known to have bathed trimonthly—a sophisticated woman. Her attendants proudly claimed that she "hath a bath every three months whether she needeth it or no." Perfume was generally used to squelch offending odors.

Cromwell frowned on the idea of using

soap and imposed excessively punitive taxes on it, setting a precedent for his successors, who saw in soap an untapped source for revenue. Both in France and England, by either handing out monopolies or levying heavy taxes, monarchs managed to hamper the production of soap through the middle of the nineteenth century. This in spite of the fact that a number of discoveries—particularly that of Nicolas Leblanc, a chemist who found a way of making lye from common salt—could have made soap easily attainable by common folk. In England soap pots were zealously watched by tax officers, clamped closed with locked lids at nightfall lest any soap be secretly made without the government getting its due. The duty, in time, came to equal the cost of making the soap itself. Needless to say, soap must have been prohibitive to buy. It was a happy day in 1852 when the tax was abolished (a "clean nation is a happy nation," said Chancellor of the Exchequer Gladstone). Soap soon became commonly available, and washable clothes became the vogue.

In 1815 a number of poor olive harvests had induced soapers to investigate the use of oils other than olive. Parallel advances in steam navigation made access to oils from far-off ports possible. Both these situations combined were responsible for a change in the basic soap formulation from olive oil to a carefully selected blend of fats and oils, as are used today.

It is worth mentioning here that only relatively recently have people come to think of cleanliness as a positive virtue and bathing something to be considered by other than the eccentric. Bathing as a communal affair—the Greek, Roman, and Turkish baths, the baths of the Middle Ages—was only incidentally a cleaning process; it was mainly a social duty. To their credit, the Romans and Turks enjoyed it as a relaxing pastime; unfortunately it would take eighteen centuries before bathing was so appreciated again. It was yet to metamorphose into a religious affair, with bathing considered a means of removing the stains contracted by contact with sinners, disease or madness, with childbirth or people of inferior castes.

Fifteenth-century folk seem to have bathed, but by the seventeenth century bathing was unheard of. In the eighteenth and early nineteenth centuries it regained some vogue as a medical or restorative treatment. Water was considered a strange magical fluid which if incorrectly applied might cause disaster, but when administered by a doctor was proven beneficial for all manner of infestation: "Preternatural Thirst, All Sorts of Worms, and Disorders of the Stomach and Intemperance."

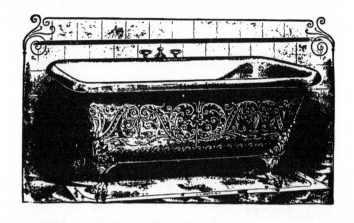

As more doctors prescribed the water cure, the idea of bathing slowly became acceptable. Not without a measure of fear, people tried bathing and found it, to their surprise, a pleasure in its own right. The popularization of the nonmedical bath happily coincided with the repeal of the soap taxes and other restrictions inhibiting its manufacture. With the increasing availability of soap and a new fondness for bathing, at long last Europe was on the verge of attaining a degree of cleanliness that was known to ancient peoples and "savages."

Advances in plumbing, particularly hot-and-cold running water and bathtubs that drained and no longer had to be baled out, took soap over its last hurdle—into the house and by the sink for good.

Soap manufacture thrived in England. England's oldest firm, Pears, was joined by several other manufacturers, some, like

Yardley and Lever Brothers, still known to-day. Soon milling equipment and other soap machinery that had originated in France was being exported throughout Europe and the New World. Indeed soap had entered the modern era.

AND WHAT OF SOAP IN AMERICA?

AS SOAP was not here when they arrived, the early settlers were obliged to make it themselves. The American Indians, who had a much higher regard for bathing than their new white neighbors, kept clean without the use of soap. (It is said that the Indians were slow in adopting English clothing because their women couldn't get it clean.) The Indians may have used some saponaceous (soap-like) botanicals like fuchsia leaves, yucca root, soap bark, bouncing bet, soaproot, and the small agave.

Making soap, as far as the settlers were concerned, was women's business. And quite a business it was. The women stored up left-over cooking grease and animal fat all year long for soapmaking day, a yearly event that preceded spring cleaning. Ashes from the fireplaces also had to be stored in order to make the lye. The lye was made in a wooden log that had been hollowed out to form a basin. A few holes cut through the bottom served as a drain. The tub was filled with ashes—hardwood ashes were considered preferable to pine or beech. Straw, twigs, and sticks lined the tub and kept ashes from sifting out. Rainwater was trickled through the ashes to leach out the lye (the potassium salts that the ashes contained) into a waiting receptacle. A fresh egg was used to determine whether the lye was of proper strength. If it sank ever so slowly, all was well. If it floated, the lye was thought to be too strong, and would have to be diluted; if it dropped, the lye was too weak, and would be run through the "ash hopper" again or boiled down.

Solid fats would have to be rendered, and then all fats boiled and skimmed to rid it of extraneous hair, dirt, spices, and other debris. Then it would all be strained through a fine cloth. The lye was then stirred into the fats, and the process, once begun, might last all day. If it worked, swell. If it separated, one tried again.

It was a lengthy procedure, all in all, and the result was somewhat crude. Home-leached lye made a soft soap, a liquid soap, though hard soaps were occasionally made, perhaps with the addition of special ingredients. Soft or hard, it sufficed, and for the next 365 days one could forget such indignities and go on to some other arduous household task.

One hundred and fifty years of this and at last some enterprising fellows decided to take the task off the housewive's hands. The women were dubious, but on the whole soapmaking was a task they were not loath to relinquish. These early soap entrepreneurs made rounds of local households, bought up fat, made soap from it, and sold the soap back to the housewives. They were called Tallow Chandlers and Soap Boilers. One such gentleman placed the following ad in the July 27, 1776, *Virginia Gazette:*

> *The subscriber (lately from Norfolk) begs leave to inform the Publick, that he has erected a manufactory of SOAP & CANDLES in this City, and intends carrying on his business in the best manner. He will give 7d halfpenny a pound for tallow, 12d for myrtle wax, 2s, 6d for picked cotton, and 1s for tow wick; for wood ashes 7d halfpenny per bushel, and 1s, 3d for tobacco ashes. He begs the inhabitants in and about the city to be careful of their ashes, as he shall be able to supply them with good soap cheaper than they can make it in their families.*

At that time soap and candles were considered kindred trades, both being made with tallow.

The soap was at first peddled door to door; eventually it found its way into general stores, where it was sold from enormous blocks. You would indicate how much you wanted, and that amount would be cut off and tucked into your shopping basket to be carried home. The soap came in two varieties: mottled brown (made with resin—a filler and extender) and a finer white variety that secured a higher price.

In 1806 one William Colgate opened up a soapmaking concern in New York called Colgate & Company. He bought himself a soap kettle that could make 45,000-pound batches (his colleagues thought it madness). Colgate & Company was to become the first great soap manufacturer in this country, though it was not until the 1830's that the concern began selling individually wrapped

bars in uniform weights. In 1872 Colgate came out with Cashmere Bouquet, a perfumed toilet soap that was a milestone in the company's history. Engineering advances as well as discoveries in soap technology had made soapmaking a science that could be carried out on increasingly larger scales. (Remember Monsieur Lablanc? There was also a Monsieur Chevreul; he was responsible for figuring out what, in fact, took place in the soap pot.)

About this time, William Procter and James Gamble—one a soaper, the other a candlemaker, and married to two sisters—set up business together in Cincinnati. From selling candles and soaps house to house off a wheelbarrow, the business grew, and soon all steamers that touched in at Cincinnati carried off boxes of Procter & Gamble products to points up and down the river—Pittsburgh, Memphis, Louisville. Their real breakthrough came in 1875, when an absentminded Procter & Gamble employee left his crutcher (soap mixer) on during his lunch break, thereby beating quantities of air into the batch and producing, quite accidentally, the first floating soap. The foreman wanted the soap reboiled, but management thought they might have something there, and lo and behold they did. Next they needed a name. Harley Procter, son of the original Procter, inspired one church Sunday by the reading of the forty-fifth psalm—"All thy garments smell of myrrh, and aloes, and cassia, out of the ivory palaces, whereby they have made thee glad"—christened the white soap Ivory. The first cake of Ivory was sold in July, 1879.

Out West, the B.J. Johnson Company was making a soap entirely of vegetable oils—palm and olive (also cocoa butter). The soap was popular enough for them to rename their company after it—Palmolive. Today's Palmolive Soap is not the same as the original.

In Kansas, the Peet Brothers pooled their combined capital to make 500 dollars and started their own factory, which was to become a great business institution of the West.

Lever Brothers, an English firm, sent over some of their staff to get things started in the U.S., and came out with Lifebuoy in 1895. Lifebuoy was sold as an antiseptic soap at first, and didn't do well until they changed its name to Lifebuoy Health Soap, got rid of the carbolic odor that made it smell so antiseptic, and invented B.O.

The Peet Brothers merged with Palmolive to become Palmolive-Peet, and in 1928 joined the Colgate Company to create the Colgate-Palmolive-Peet Company. (In 1953 Peet was dropped from the title, leaving us with Colgate-Palmolive.)

With the introduction of our cast of characters we come to the end of the first phase of soap history in this country. Thereafter the soap story becomes the history of a multibillion-dollar industry. We now find ourselves with strong established companies, very competitive, each bent on making their particular products leaders in the field.

From the beginning, the competition was aided and abetted by a nascent advertising industry which could be said, in turn, to have "cut its teeth" on soap. The post-Civil War boom of the seventies, eighties, and nineties brought with it a plethora of advertising gimmicks: gold dollars and five-cent pieces tucked into select bars; soap cards with pinup girls sporting the latest modes—high-button shoes, high collars, high hairdos. Showgirls "from the New York stage" were recruited to tout their favorite brands. Soap packages began to appear in colors and were weighted with text—copy not only on the outside of the wrapper but on the inside, too. Page-long ads in tiny type left not one potential quality of a product unheralded. This, as you might imagine, was before advertising discovered that it could sell a product without any mention of its virtues. These late-nineteenth-century ads are fascinating to read. Ivory ads, for some reason, were always different, rather sophisticated and ahead of their time. Ivory was probably the first product to use slogans in advertising (It floats! 99 44/100% pure!). Following their lead, slogans replaced the lengthy descriptive sales pitch, and by the turn of the century had become *the* advertising medium. Magazines,

After you have given the grocer's man your order for tea, sugar, flour, coffee, biscuit, breakfast food, eggs, and vegetables, add "And a quarter's worth of Ivory Soap."

Ivory Soap is the handiest thing you can have around the house.

You can use it in the bathroom, in the washroom, in every bedroom, in the kitchen, and in the laundry. There is no better soap than Ivory — none which is at once so economical, so pure, or which can be used for so many different purposes.

A WORD OF WARNING — There are many white soaps, each represented to be as good as Ivory; they are not, but like all imitations they lack the peculiar and remarkable qualities of the genuine. Ask for Ivory Soap and insist upon getting it.

Ivory Soap ~ 99 44/100 Per Cent. Pure.

as a vehicle for ads, became the great soap popularizer, a role that the radio would eventually claim for its own (soap operas).

Soon readily dissolvable and quick-sudsing flake and granulated soaps came on the market, giving advertisers that many more products to promote. Lever Brothers brought out Lux in 1906. Procter & Gamble brought out Ivory Flakes and Ivory Snow. Colgate came out with Fab. These flake soaps replaced the cake soap for washing fine fabrics. Lever brought out the first granulated laundry soap to swoop in on the burgeoning washing machine business. Soon the condition of the family wash became a subject of serious attention. Testimonials of local housewives proclaimed that "Rinso cleans whiter."

It wasn't long before advertising came upon its best ploy: the scare technique. Lifebuoy's 1926 B.O. campaign typified it. It was a particularly effective tack. "Perspiration odor" had become "body odor" which now became "B.O." Like Listerine, which made halitosis the social disease of the twenties and thirties, soap ads fed on one's fear of imminent social ostracism. Lost jobs or declined promotions, bad grades, broken engagements, no date on Saturday night, irritable mates—you name it—all were considered the fault of those unwise enough not to use the product. So effective was Lifebuoy's ad campaign that a whole generation of kids grew up knowing no more potent invective than "You've got B.O."

Here soap is the bridge between the reader and the genteel world of lawn sport and white linen.

Linen is a more elegant material than cotton for summer dress. Linen will look like cotton if washed with any but Ivory Soap.

There is no "free" (uncombined oil or alkali in Ivory Soap The combination is complete Containing no 'free oil ' it rinses perfectly There being no ' free alkali, it is harmless to for skin or fabric 99⁴⁴/₁₀₀ per cent pure It floats.

*One of the early pre-
mium offers and
quite a brainstorm it
was—to have the
consumer carry
around with him at
all times a replica of
the product.*

THE IVORY SOAP
WATCH CHARMS.

A miniature fac-simile of a cake of Ivory Soap,
with a gold-plated ring to attach it to the watch
chain, or may be tied to the button-hole with a
piece of ribbon, and used as a badge for a club,
society, etc., etc.

HOW TO GET ONE FOR NOTHING

Save the outside wrappers of Ivory Soap, and
when you have twelve, cut out the center piece
of each wrapper and send them to us (as per
directions below), and we will send you, by
mail, one of the Watch Charms. If you are
not now using Ivory Soap, buy twelve cakes,
and you will get full value for your money in
soap, and the watch charm for nothing.

FOLLOW THESE DIRECTIONS.

Cut out the center piece of each wrapper
and put them in the envelope with your
letter, saying what you want, and give your
address in full. *No attention will be paid
to requests for Watch Charms unless the
twelve (12) center pieces are in the envelope
with the request.*

PROCTER & GAMBLE, CINCINNATI, OHIO.

(Please mention this paper.)

Late nineteenth century ads used animals for their sentimental pull. Is it the monkey that makes this picture so disquieting?

Pears' Soap

"MATCHLESS FOR THE COMPLEXION."

More animals—this time enjoying a slide show. Its appeal to whimsy is rather low-keyed and sophisticated compared to other ads of the time.

The evolution of the Procter & Gamble trademark.

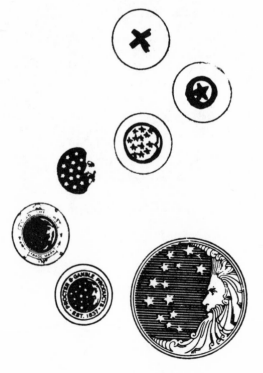

A study in cultural attitudes in an 1880's ad: both Indian and environment are reduced to billboards.

This 1885 ad is the written equivalent of the carnival pitch-man weaving a spell through the power of words. Here the pro-duct is soap rather than snake oil. No potential user or use of the soap is left un-named.

A social success ad in which the product assures "a simply perfect evening" and "another . . . soon."

A maiden saved from the sin of middle-age skin—with redemption accomplished in only three comic-strip frames. (Soap advertisers of the thirties discovered in the comic-strip format a vivid and accessible means of instant communication.)

In the thirties one could never go too far to track down perspiration odor. Considering all that could go wrong, it's a wonder people ever left their houses.

Surely one of the most famous soap slogans. The original illustration is in magnificent color—softly tinted and tenderly romantic.

You too, can have the charm of
"A Skin you love to touch"

THE beautiful fresh clear skin you long for—with the right care you can possess it!

Any girl can have a smooth, flawless complexion.

Each day your skin is changing—old skin dies and new takes its place. This new skin you can make what you will!

If you are troubled with blackheads—with ugly little blemishes—with conspicuous nose pores; if your skin is too oily, or so pale and sallow that it gives your whole face a lifeless appearance—begin now, to overcome that condition.

Give your skin the right Woodbury treatment for its needs, and see how easy it is to free your complexion from the faults that have been troubling you.

The right Woodbury treatment for each type of skin and its needs is given in the booklet around every cake of Woodbury's Facial Soap.

Get a cake of Woodbury's today and begin your treatment tonight. Within a week or ten days you will notice a marked improvement in your complexion.

The same qualities that give Woodbury's its beneficial effect in overcoming common skin troubles make it ideal for regular toilet use. A 25-cent cake lasts a month or six weeks.

A complete miniature set of the Woodbury skin preparations

For 25 cents we will send you a complete miniature set of the Woodbury skin preparations, containing:

A trial size cake of Woodbury's Facial Soap.
A sample tube of the new Woodbury's Facial Cream.
A sample tube of Woodbury's Cold Cream.
A sample box of Woodbury's Facial Powder.
Together with the treatment booklet, "A Skin You Love to Touch"

Address The Andrew Jergens Co., 305 Spring Grove Ave., Cincinnati, Ohio. If you live in Canada, address The Andrew Jergens Co., Limited, 305 Sherbrooke St., Perth, Ontario. English Agents: H. C. Quelch & Co., 4 Ludgate Square, London, E. C. 4.

WOODBURY'S FACIAL SOAP

*Today's enzyme-
active lemon-
freshened boraxed
megapowder was
once but a simple
coconut-oil soap
flake, the product il-
lustrated in this
lovely ad.*

Babes in the Woois

All through the winter, babes play out-of-doors
wrapped snug and warm in furs and wools.
Caps, coats and leggings go forth each day as
clean and comfortable as the mothers' loving
care can make them.

To help mothers keep warm winter wraps clean,
Colgate & Co. have made Fab — cocoanut-oil
soap flakes.

The cocoanut-oil in Fab makes the tiny flakes
dissolve like snowflakes in warm water. No bits
of soap can stay in Fab-suds to stick to woolly
threads and shrink or mat them.

Fab-suds bring back the snowy white to mittens,
leggings and sweaters. Fab-suds wash softly the
little frock and flannels beneath.

Over 115 years' experience in making fine soaps
has gone into the production of FAB. No effort
was spared to make these cocoanut-oil flakes
safe for children's clothes.

COLGATE & CO.
Fu 1806
NEW YORK

A color print, for framing, of this Neida (H. Willebeek Le Mair) painting for six . cents. in stamps.

Working for a soap company in the twenties seems to have been a not unpleasant proposition. A new breed of "benevolent" bosses felt profit sharing and annual employee picnics the least a company could do to promote the happiness and good cheer of its workers. Lever Brothers' eleventh annual employee outing in July of 1927 was quite a fest. Two silver cups were awarded for obstacle golf, and in a closely contested ball game between office staff and workers, the office team won, 4-3. There was dancing during the day with music provided by Morely Pearl's Boston Orchestra; also concerts given by the Stiles Military Band. Can you see them in the band shell? It seems a good deal of fun was had by all.

Litigation was another activity that seems to have occupied a good deal of the soap manufacturers' energies. There were innumerable in-industry suits, and a lot of trouble from the Federal Trade Commission.

A glimpse at some high drama on the legal front: In 1927 Andrew Jergens Company was on Woodbury's back for having come out with a similar product Woodbury had sold Jergens the rights to manufacture some twenty-five years earlier. Jergens charged that the new soap was not a "Genuine Imported Pure Castile Soap" as advertised, that its wrapper was a colorable imitation of the Jergens' wrapper around their "John H. Woodbury Facial Soap," and that the new Woodbury company had incorporated itself for the sole purpose of cashing in on the reputation of Jergens soap.

What in fact determined what could rightfully be called a Castile soap happened to be a subject of unending debate near and dear to the hearts of many in the soap and allied industries. A number of soap companies had soaps labeled Castile on the market, some made with olive oil, some not. Olive oil importers, determined not to let anyone get away with calling a soap Castile if it wasn't made with their product, were the first to raise the issue of what was a "genuine" Castile soap.

What determined a "genuine" naptha soap was also in question. About the same time as the Jergens-Woodbury war was raging, the Federal Trade Commission was giving Procter & Gamble a hard time about labeling a soap "naphtha" if it primarily contained kerosene or less than one percent by weight of naphtha (naphtha being a more efficient cleaning agent than kerosene). Naphtha was to the twenties' soapmaker what enzymes were to be to the detergent maker of the sixties.

Colgate was having its troubles too, not with a rival company or the government, but with one Miss Ella C. Patterson of Milwaukee. Miss Patterson, a niece of General

Ambrose E. Burnside of Civil War fame, sued Colgate for using the general's picture to advertise its shaving soap. Colgate won.

Lever Brothers and Procter & Gamble were politely at one another's throats, where they would remain for a good number of years. The battle began with Lever's Rinso, the granulated soap which had been a leader in its field since its introduction in 1919. In the late twenties, Lever started making Rinso by a new process which turned out (in 1937) to be a patent infringement. They were obliged to pay Procter & Gamble (and Colgate) five million dollars. This did not make Lever too happy. Nor was Procter & Gamble too happy when Lever came out with the vegetable shortening Spry to compete with Procter & Gamble's long-standing Crisco.

In 1940 Lever acquired a patent on a new secret revolutionary continuous manufacturing technique for making a new floating soap called Swan. Not so secret a process, it seemed, when in a month Procter & Gamble came out with a "new Ivory," also made by the continuous process. Lever claimed a patent infringement and sued. Procter & Gamble countersued with an injunction against sales of Swan as an evident imitation of Ivory. Ivory then jazzed up its black-on-white wrapper to white-on-blue after Swan's white-on-green started attracting attention.

Battle was waged in magazine ads throughout the country. Accusations of theft and espionage echoed in industry channels. Procter & Gamble felt unfairly treated; after all, they had left the B.O. market (Lifebuoy) to Lever. Floating soap was theirs! Years later, Procter & Gamble came out with Zest, their own deodorant bar.

THE INTRODUCTION of synthetic detergents brings us up to modern day and is responsible for changing the entire face and shape of the soap industry. Germany had had some success with synthetic detergents during World War I, when the scarcity of raw materials created a need for an alternate way of making soap. In the U.S. a gentleman by the name of Lawrence F. Flett investigated the possibility and became convinced that synthetic detergents would revolutionize the industry. He spoke at soap industry meetings and conventions, but like most visionaries was not taken seriously. Nothing, it was felt, would ever replace soap, as it was the best of all possible cleansers.

Come World War II, animal and vegetable oils were in low supply and there was little soap to be had. Housewives were asked to save their fats, as they did in the old days. The Navy, in particular, was in dire need of large quantities of soap that just were not available. Scientists were at last obliged to investigate the possibility of substituting mineral oils for animal fats and vegetable oils. They found that an acid similar to fatty acid (the compound present in animal fats and vegetable oils; here it is necessary to stop thinking of acids as substances that burn) could be made from petroleum chemicals reacted with sulphuric acid. Combined with an alkali similar to lye, this new compound made a synthetic cleaning agent that was even good in hard (mineral-rich) water.

By the end of the war the new detergents were being used extensively in industry, particularly in the textile field. Popular acceptance was not long in coming, and soon synthetic detergents replaced soap for all manner of household laundering and cleaning. Colgate and Lever were late in getting into the detergent market, but Procter & Gamble was not. Procter & Gamble had brought out a synthetic detergent called Dreft in the thirties with little success; but when they brought out Tide in 1947—a more propitious time—they virtually took over the entire soap and detergent field, securing for themselves a place in the industry that remains to this day unrivaled.

So there you have it. With synthetic dishwashing detergents, washing machine detergents, shampoos, household cleansers of all kinds, only a small percentage of the soap industry is now involved with our old faithful bar of toilet soap. The standard formula for almost all toilet soaps now made is 80/20—eighty percent tallow and about twenty percent coconut oil.

HOW TO USE SOAP

THERE WAS A TIME when a bar of soap was a most luxurious oddity. Soap might be sent cross-continent as a gift of goodwill from one influential party to another—just as jewels were sent earlier this century and pandas nowadays. In the late seventeenth century a German princess received a present of soap from an Italian emissary, accompanied by a detailed description of how it was to be used. As I have not been able to track down the Italian's instructions, I offer some of my own.

How long your soap lasts is determined by the degree to which it is subjected to water. If you hold the soap under the tap, it will not last long. Instead, you should wet your hands, rub them about the dry bar of soap, return the soap to the soap dish, work up a lather, wash, and rinse. If Americans did this, they would use sixty percent less soap and be none the less clean.

Special Soaps

FOR THOSE OF YOU whom success motivates to further heights, there are indeed reaches of soap-fancy still to be explored. There are additional ingredients that can be added to make your soap even richer. There are possibilities of color and scent yet untapped. You might also like to experiment with interesting shapes and molds. Here are some ideas for specialty soaps and some general instructions that may help you create your own. Because all involve additional factors, steps or techniques, it would make sense to embark on these only after you have successfully handled one or more of the basic soaps.

COCOABUTTER SOAP

COCOABUTTER IS a nutrient and an emollient. Adding it to your soap makes the soap superfatted. It comes in eight-ounce bars that are divided into one-ounce fingers. Melt two fingers in a double boiler or in a hot water bath. Do not overheat. Add it to your soap pot just prior to pouring the soap into molds. Mix well.

SOLID SHAMPOO BAR

A FINE SHAMPOO bar, it eliminates the need for a conditioner. Squeeze the juice of a lemon into a bottle and add water to it for your final rinse. This soap will not wash away natural oils.

> 24 ounces coconut oil   12 ounces lye
> 38 ounces olive oil   32 ounces water
> 24 ounces castor oil

SUPERFATTED OLIVE OIL SOAP

YOU CAN ADD two extra ounces of olive oil to any recipe prior to pouring the soap into molds. The two ounces should be mixed in well; they will not saponify but will blend into newly formed soap, making a rich and creamy product. This soap could be used as a makeup remover.

COLD CREAM SOAP

ADD TWO OUNCES of any cold cream to your soap prior to pouring the soap into molds. This addition in particular must be mixed in very well. Cold Cream Soap will soften the skin and remove imbedded deposits of dirt.

BUTTER ENRICHED SOAP

USE ANY RECIPE that has coconut oil in it and replace a quarter of the amount of coconut oil with butter when you weigh in your fats. Though butter may reduce the foaming power of your soap, it makes a very mild, pleasing bar.

HEALTH BAR　　　IF YOUR INTEREST is in health foods and vitamins, try a Health Bar. Add wheat germ oil or your favorite vitamin. Wheat germ oil superfats a soap. Vitamin E is a mild deodorizer. Other vitamins would be considered nutrients. Add two ounces (liquid) prior to pouring. Mix well.

MILK AND HONEY SOAP　　　MIX TOGETHER one ounce each of powdered milk and honey. Add to your soap prior to pouring, and mix well. This soap could have been Cleopatra's favorite.

ROSEWATER SOAP　　　WHEN PREPARING the lye solution, add four ounces less water in which to dissolve the lye. When the lye solution has cooled, add four ounces of rosewater and mix. Rosewater is dilute and its scent won't hold; however, you should get its properties which are astringent. For scent, add three-quarters to one ounce of essential oils—rose and perhaps a woody note, another floral and an animal essence to sophisticate it.

**ALMOND
MEAL
SOAP**

ALMOND MEAL is a good degreaser. It is ever so gently abrasive and good at removing imbedded dirt from pores. Use an ounce of it in the Castile Soap if you have oily skin. Use any of the other soaps if oiliness is not a problem. Oatmeal and cornmeal can be used, too; and pumice, but only as a hand cleanser. Don't use sand. Add prior to pouring in the molds, and mix well.

**SUPERFATTED
LANOLIN
SOAP**

ADD TWO OUNCES of anhydrous (water-free) deodorized lanolin to your soap prior to pouring it in the molds. Deodorized lanolin is important because otherwise the oil smells just like the sheep from whose wool it comes. If you have trouble finding it at your drugstore, try a chemical supply house. Lanolin has all the characteristics of a good night cream. Melt it in a double boiler and keep it warm.

**PETROLEUM
DANDRUFF
SHAMPOO
BAR**

PEOPLE WHO work in oil fields never have dandruff, as the oil lubricates their hair and combats dryness. Try an ounce each of deodorized kerosene and castor oil, pre-mixed. Add to your soap and stir well prior to pouring. Rinse with lemon water (see SOLID SHAMPOO BAR).

DRY HAIR SHAMPOO BAR

Add to the Vegetable Soap an ounce and a half each of glycerin and castor oil, premixed, prior to pouring. Rinse with lemon water (see SOLID SHAMPOO BAR).

1½ T = 1½ oz

AVOCADO SOAP

Using the Castile Soap recipe, replace six ounces of olive oil with avocado oil when weighing in the fats. This one is for sensitive skins.

One is forever tempted to introduce fruits or vegetables into the soap mixture. Peaches for a peach soap. Avocado for an avocado soap. Don't do it; it doesn't work. The lye will transmogrify fresh fruits and vegetables, not to mention the disruption solid matter added to your soap might cause. If you want, you can add peach kernel *oil* or avocado *oil;* that's another matter.

Oils not called for in the recipes can be introduced as superfatting agents or as replacements. Superfatting agents are oils that are in excess to the formula. They do not become saponified and are considered enrichments to the soap. All superfatting agents should be added to your soap right before you are ready to pour it into the molds. They should be stirred in well. If you want to divide your batch and try something different with each half, try splitting your ready-to-pour soap into two bowls; add the additional ingredients, stir, then pour into the molds. Stirring in the molds is clumsy; one can never quite get at it. If you experiment with additions not covered in this book, add no more than an ounce or two, which is sufficient. Additional ingredients may slow the soap's solidification by a day.

To make replacements in recipes, weigh in the ingredient with the rest of the fats prior to saponification. Use no more than a few ounces, and use an equal amount less of one of the oils in the recipe.

Another way of introducing special properties into your soap is by making a strong tea of whatever herb, spice, fruit or vegetable interests you, and using it to replace part of the water used to dissolve the lye. You won't get the scent, but you should get the properties. Some possibilities might be:

FOR DRY SKIN SOAPS

acacia	elder flower
clover	melilot
cowslips	slippery elm bark

FOR OILY SKIN SOAPS

cucumber	witch hazel
rose	

FOR ASTRINGENT SOAPS

camomile   strawberry

FOR A SHAMPOO SOAP FOR BLONDES

camomile   marigold
mullein flowers

FOR A SHAMPOO SOAP FOR BRUNETTES

rosemary   red sage
raspberry leaf

To make the tea, pour boiling water over whatever ingredient you are using. Cover and let steep for about a day. Then strain off the solid materials, reserving the water. Make your lye solution with four to ten ounces less water than called for in the recipe. When the lye solution has cooled down some, add tea in an amount equivalent to the water you have omitted. Stir.

On Scenting

THE FRENCH, as one would imagine, were the first to scent soap. It was the perfumers, not the soapmakers, who established this art. Perfumers would buy soap in slabs. Then they would shred the soap into chips and place them in mixers, where the perfume was added. To homogenize the perfume with the soap, the soap was passed through roller mills. It was then compacted in a device somewhat like a meat grinder, from which it emerged looking like a thick sausage. The final stage was pressing the soap into cakes. The use of rollers to introduce perfume into soap has become known as French milling.

When it comes to adding fragrance to homemade soap, it is best to think in terms of scenting it, not perfuming it. Not because of the process, but because of the art. Perfuming is a rather inaccessible art, complex and difficult for the uninitiate. By perfuming I mean the creation of fragrances that are sometimes reminiscent of but usually unlike anything in nature; that are alluring and memorable in not quite definable ways. Perfumes, the ones you own, are made of dozens of ingredients put together in the most intricate and thoughtful manner: thought is given to which scent is smelled first (the most volatile), which will bolster the main idea, which will hold the fragrance intact and keep it from changing. One ingredient is used to push another up, one to hold another down; one to add a spicy note, another to add an herbal note; one to sophisticate a fragrance; one to round them all up and form the bouquet. There are top notes and base notes, woody notes and citrus notes, semicitrus and floral notes, and others quite indescribable. So let us leave perfume to books on the subject and investigate simpler manners of scenting soap.

The best way to scent soap is to add a fragrant essential oil. Essential oils are the essences of fragrances. They are obtained from flowers, herbs, woods, spices, roots, resins, lichens, mosses—all categories of growing things. They are obtained through a number of processes: distillation, expression, maceration, and absorption, which the French call enfleurage. There are animal essences, too, and these are obtained in an equal number of ways, most of which are unspeakable. You can purchase essential oils, such as oil of lavender and oil of musk, at your pharmacies, health food stores, herb shops, and perfumery suppliers—their availability increases daily. They are usually purchased by the half ounce or ounce and can be quite expensive—from fifty cents a half ounce to twenty dollars and up. Thyme and rosemary are less expensive than, say tuberose and oleander. Some are so expensive, such as a true oil of rose, that synthetic oils are the only ones available and feasible for the general public. These will do, as you have no alternative. If you have trouble finding an oil you want locally, you can mail-order it from any number of places. Among my favorite suppliers are Caswell-Massey Co. Ltd., Lexington Avenue at 48th Street, New York, New York 10017; Indiana Botanic Gardens, P.O. Box 5, Hammond, Indiana 46325; and Aphrodisia Products, 28 Carmine Street, New York, New York 10014. You might just send away for their catalogues whether you need an oil or not as they are an absolute pleasure to peruse. Caswell-Massey's catalogue is free and it may be the loveliest catalogue published anywhere. Indiana Botanic Gardens sends out a charming almanac, also free. Aphrodisia's catalogue costs one dollar.

Expect anything you add to your soap mixture to smell somewhat differently when the soap has hardened. All oils are affected in some way by the lye component of the soap—it will change some oils imperceptibly, others entirely. Hard-and-fast rules as to what works well and what doesn't are hard to give; oils vary considerably, depending on where and when they were bought, where the flowers or herbs or spices or whatever grew, when they were picked, whether the sun was high or the rain intense, whether the oil has been doctored some. This is not an area of absolutes. Try—you will certainly find something to your liking.

Here are some oils you might consider. Bayberry is spicy and might appeal to men. Sandalwood is luxurious, soft, and woody. Cyclamen is very floral and sweet. Patchouli is woody and musty. Rosemary fresh and light and herbal. Oakmoss is green and woody, and helps cover the fatty base of a soap. Ylang-ylang is a poor man's jasmine, and of course jasmine, which is sweet and narcotic.

Bitter almond I like particularly. Add a little oil of musk to sweeten it and bring up its scent, and maybe a little cedarwood to cover the fatty base.

Carnation is spicy and could go with bayberry, bay, and clove to make a spice soap. Add a wee bit of bergamot, or petit-grain, which are considered semicitrus, and a small amount of calamus to add a whis-keylike note.

Styrax I can't quite describe. A little bit of it and some jasmine might bring up the honey scent in the Milk and Honey Soap. It is balsamic and somewhat spicy. It hasn't much to offer on its own, but might be good mixed with either coumarin or ylang-ylang.

You can use oil of rose—some people are devoted to it, others don't like the scent divorced from the flower. Mixed with some woody notes (sandalwood, a little oakmoss and patchouli), a few other florals like gardenia and jasmine or ylang-ylang, some cyclamen, a little lavender for spiciness, and you should have a very nice floral scent.

Gardenia is a very, very heavy floral. Bay is spicy, as is lavender, but not in the same way. Vetiver and cedarwood are two useful woody notes.

All of these oils should hold in your soap. You can use one alone, or two or three, or as many as you care to. Some mixed scents, like Russian Leather, New Mown Grass, and Fresh Cut Hay, are also available at the same outlets as these oils.

Less expensive and less sophisticated are the flavor extracts you use in the kitchen. You can try them. If you want an elaborate and established scent, you could try your own perfume, though it will be an expensive experiment. Do not use toilet waters or cologne.

For all the soap recipes in this book, try three-quarters of an ounce or four and a half teaspoons of scent material. After you have tried three-quarters, you can decide whether more or less is to your liking. If you are measuring by spoonful, use standard measuring spoons.

If you want to try multi-ingredient scent recipes, you may need an eyedropper. There are about 450 drops in three-quarters of an ounce. An eyedropper fills up about halfway with one squeeze—that's about twenty drops. Measure by droppersful to save the tedious counting of drops. A dropperful equals twenty drops.

Try not to adulterate your oils by introducing the same unwashed eyedropper into different scents. Do your best to keep the scents pure. Water itself won't clean off the oils, as they are not water soluble. Rubbing alcohol will. Rinse the dropper in alcohol after each measuring bout by squeezing some in, then out. Try to accurately estimate as much as you need so you won't have to return excess oil to the bottle.

The following are recipes for soap scents culled from different sources—some tried, some untried. Feel free to experiment with them.

LINNET

Oil of bitter almond	16 *droppersful and* 5 *drops*
Oil of bergamot	6 *droppersful and* 11 *drops*
Oil of lemon	4 *droppersful and* 7 *drops*

KRESS

Oil of lemon	3 *droppersful and* 13 *drops*
Oil of bergamot	1 *dropperful and* 6 *drops*
Oil of lavender ....14 *droppersful and* 14 *drops*
Oil of neroli	3 *droppersful and* 13 *drops*
Oil of peppermint	15 *drops*
Oil of verbena	1 *dropperful and* 16 *drops*
Oil of cinnamon	7 *drops*

LUNA

Oil of lemon ....7 *droppersful*
Oil of lavender ....5 *droppersful*
Oil of peppermint ....5 *droppersful*
Oil of sage ....4 *droppersful*
Oil of rosemary ....4 *droppersful*
Oil of cinnamon ....3 *droppersful*

CHAMMY

Oil of bergamot ....2 *droppersful and 14 drops*
Oil of lemon ....6 *droppersful and 11 drops*
Oil of neroli ....7 *droppersful and 14 drops*
Oil of sweet orange ....7 *droppersful and 14 drops*
Oil of rosemary ....2 *droppersful and 14 drops*

SATURDAY BLEND

Oil of cinnamon ....11 *droppersful and 9 drops*
Oil of cassia ....5 *droppersful and 14 drops*
Oil of sassafras ....4 *droppersful and 11 drops*
Oil of bergamot ....4 *droppersful and 11 drops*

COROLLA

Oil of bergamot ....25 *droppersful*
Oil of lemon ....17 *drops*
Oil of neroli .... 4 *drops*
Oil of rosemary .... 2 *drops*
Oil of lavender .... 2 *drops*
Oil of musk .... 4 *drops*

SEEDS

Oil of fennel ....18 *droppersful and 10 drops*
Oil of caraway .... 8 *droppersful and 10 drops*

PAPER AND VELVET

Oil of bergamot ....10 *droppersful*
Oil of lavender .... 8 *droppersful and 6 drops*
Oil of thyme .... 4 *droppersful*
Oil of coumarin .... 3 *droppersful and 6 drops*
Oil of musk .... 1 *dropperful and 13 drops*

AUTHOR'S OWN

Oil of jasmine .... 5 *droppersful*
Oil of ylang-ylang .... 5 *droppersful*
Oil of gardenia .... 2 *droppersful*
Oil of lavender .... 4 *droppersful*
Oil of rosemary .... 2 *droppersful*

Oil of clove .... 1 *dropperful and 10 drops*
Oil of rose .... 1 *dropperful*
Oil of geranium bourbon ....10 *drops*
Oil of sandalwood ....16 *drops*
Oil of vetiver ....16 *drops*
Oil of patchouli ....16 *drops*
Oil of oakmoss ....16 *drops*
Oil of bergamot .... 1 *dropperful and 10 drops*
Oil of petitgrain .... 1 *dropperful and 10 drops*

SISALY

Oil of rosemary ....20 *droppersful*
Oil of lavender .... 7 *droppersful*

Scent material should be weighed and ready so that it can be added without delay right before you pour the soap mixture into the molds. Wait until the mixture traces, then add the oils and mix well. Do mix well. A slotted spoon works better than a solid one for this purpose.

On Color

IF YOUR AIM in finding a coloring agent is to avoid chemical intrusion, you can use natural dyes such as cocoa, or the spice turmeric, or chlorophyll (from the druggist). There are plenty of possibilities. Many coloring agents, like these, can be simply stirred into the soap prior to pouring the soap into molds. When using a powder, make sure all particles are thoroughly dissolved in the soap. To avoid clumps, pre-mix the powder with a little soap, then stir the dyed soap back into the batch.

Think about fruits and vegetables and other plants, also roots, barks, leaves, and flowers as sources of color. As you cannot add anything solid to your soap (whatever you add has to be readily soluble), what you do is extract the color from the solid material. Make a tea by pouring boiling water over it and letting it steep until you have extracted a color that looks intense enough for dying. Strain out the solid pieces and reserve the water. If you are trying to extract color from vegetables, use fresh vegetables, not canned, as salt and other additives can interfere with the dispersement of color.

There are two ways of introducing your

colored tea into the soap and both have been known to work and not work. One is to use the tea in place of water when preparing the lye solution. (Dissolve the lye in less water than called for in the recipe and when the lye solution has cooled, make up the difference in the water requirement with colored tea.) Be forewarned: any substance added directly to lye will have to fight for its life.

The other method is to add a small portion of the colored tea—reduced by boiling to its utmost concentration—to the soap pot prior to pouring the soap into molds. The catch here is that any water added to your soap will slow its hardening process by a day. Quite simply, your soap is wetter. Try to get away with adding as little as possible; ideally, no more than an ounce. Add more and you may interfere with the soap's formulation.

No matter what method you use, the caustic element in the soap will affect all colors to some degree; some will be changed beyond recognition. The chaos the lye wreaks has its advantages though, particularly if party-colored soaps are not to your liking. What you end up with is invariably a color more subtle and interesting than the one you began with.

Artificial dyes tend to hold their own somewhat better and are easier to deal with. Candle dyes can be used (about one teaspoon directly into the soap); liquid blueing works well (use a little more); food coloring tends to form in an oil slick on top of the soap but can be forced into submission if you stir well; you can even experiment with fabric dyes.

Don't try to color the soap in the molds. Access is difficult. If you want a homogeneous color, you are better off introducing color in the soap pot or in the lye bottle. If you want to dye a single batch different colors, divide it into as many bowls as needed, and add the color there. Start with a little of the coloring agent you are using. Stir and add more as you see fit. Try to use as little as possible. Work quickly.

For a marbleized effect, gently swirl the coloring agent into the soap as you would fold melted chocolate into a marble-cake batter. I have done this successfully with blueing and cocoa. Very nice. Doesn't work with food coloring, unfortunately.

Experiment with coloring agents and techniques. Don't expect too much and you will definitely be surprised. When your soap has hardened, remember to remove the powdery layer of soda ash that envelops the bar. Lying in wait is this brilliant polished color yearning to be set free.

On Bars, Bevels, and Molds

So at last you have soap, sitting there, hardening in the molds. Perhaps it doesn't look all it should, but it will—soon—with a little more attention.

You should now have an enormous block or two of soap. Rather awesome, in its weight and bulk, isn't it? Accustomed to three-and-a-half-ounce bars, eight pounds of soap is a lot of soap. The edges of the block have been somewhat rounded by the plastic.

These have to go first, as they stand between you and perfection. With a metal spatula, a taut thin wire or a long nonserrated kitchen knife, slice off the edges to make the sides square; also slice or scrape off the powdery layer of soda ash on top. Now there's no question about it; it looks good, very good, special.

Where you take it from here is a matter of temperament and intention. What have you in mind? It would be unreproachable to just slice off slabs to use as you need them, perhaps slicing off a few extra slabs for gifts to deserving (appreciative) friends. Or to cut the block into interestingly sized bars. It would be even nicer to bevel the edges of a bar, and perhaps carve an initial into it.

To do this you need some tools. A small (six-inch) steel ruler is an excellent beveler. A small paring knife also works well. Single-edged razor blades are fine, but should only be used by those who have had some truck with them, as they can easily inflict cuts of all degrees. A metal spatula is all right, though it bends and its rounded edge is troublesome.

Cover your working area with newspaper; also cover the floor around it. Cut off a piece of soap from your block, somewhat larger than what you hope to end up with—in fact, a good deal larger, as in first attempts soap has a marked tendency to diminish in size. (You may end up with an awful lot of soap scrapings which you will just have to find some use for, like sewing them into washcloths. They tend to float to the top when reintroduced into another batch of soap.)

The squarer your bar to begin with, the finer the bevel will look in the end. By square I mean all angles should be right angles, all planes level, and all corresponding

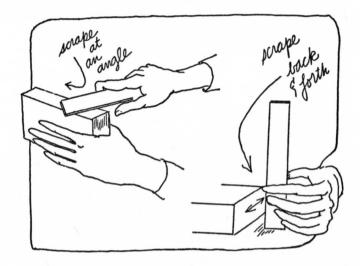

sides parallel. One secret in obtaining this end is to try not to slice. Don't approach your soap as if it were a piece of cheese. Slicing takes off too much, too quickly, too blindly. Unless you see some extreme protuberance that evidently needs to be removed with a heavy hand, the tack to take with soap is to scrape. With your straight edge, scrape lengthwise and widthwise and diagonally, as though you were scraping a carrot, but with a lighter touch. Then hold the soap firmly, and with the base of your straight edge on the tabletop, scrape back and forth. Look at your soap; not from a distance, but held a few inches from your nose. Look at it closely, really look. You can see where a side is uneven, where there is a depression or raised surface or a bump. Get rid of it. Do the corners flare out? Often they

do; straighten them out. The reason for doing all this is that bumps and depressions
will interfere with your making truly
straight beveled edges. Of course you can be
less painstaking and still end up with an
attractive bar; it depends on what degree of
refinement you feel necessary.

You will have to adjust your technique to
the consistency of the soap you are working
with. The Vegetable Soap and the Palma-
Christi Soap are on the soft side, a little
waxy. Slicing may get you further than
scrapping here, and edges will never be as
sharp as those worked in the Castile or
Copra-Olive Soap. The Castile Soap is quite
hard; it won't slice smoothly. More likely it
will crack. Scraping is fine, though. The
Copra-Olive Soap is the one I most enjoy
working with; however, they are all fine in
their own ways.

When your bar is as square as you can get
it, start beveling the edges. Hold your
straight edge at a 45-degree angle in one
hand, the soap bar in another, and scrape
away from you in one direction. (A refining
technique is to scrape up and down, also
diagonally, and from all points and angles,
turning the bar around often and not over-
emphasizing strokes in any one direction.)
Look at the soap. Again, do the corners wing
out? Get them even with the rest of the bevel. Instead of getting a smooth surface, are

you getting bumps, nicks, indentations? These may be due to uneven pressure, but more often are the result of bumps on either of the sides you are beveling. Hold the bar close, up to your nose, and you will see them. Shave them off and see if the bevel doesn't come along better.

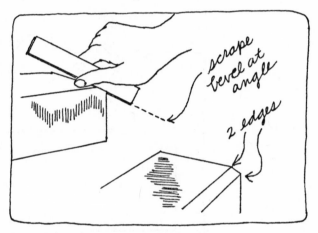

scrape bevel at angle

2 edges

Where you once had a single edge (the right angle formed by the top and side) you will now have two edges—the edges of the bevel. What about these edges? They should be straight and true. Investigate where they go awry, and fix them. You can use a ruler and pencil to mark the soap. Keep working.

A bevel can be as wide as you would like it. Between a quarter and a half inch is nice for a look that is very clean and sharp. Wider bevels are not as sharp; they don't produce the same gemlike effect, but suggest other equally interesting shapes. The softer soaps will tend toward the latter.

Bevel all four edges on the top and the four on the bottom. All bevels should be the same width. Don't fudge the corners where two beveled edges meet—they should come to a point.

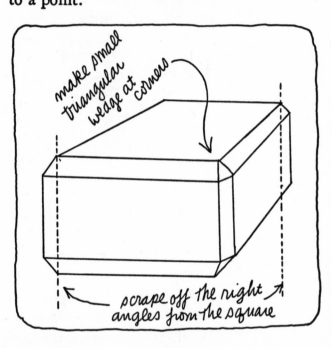

make small triangular wedge at corners

scrape off the right angles from the square

Once gotten into, it's hard to stop. So if, like the author, you can't leave well enough alone, go ahead and bevel the remaining four corners, in effect removing the last right angles from the square. And if you go this far, one last finishing touch is irresistible. Finish off these new bevels by faceting them at top and bottom. Do this by shaving off a small triangular wedge from each of eight corners involved.

The process of beveling may sound terribly complicated, but it really isn't, it is simply a matter of shaving off all the right angles of a rectangle or a cube. Fancy bars make stupendous gifts. I carve the initial of the recipient on the top of the bar, wrap it in some scrap fabric, tie it with a ribbon, and give. Often I present it with or in a soap dish; for some reason, a lovely assortment has become readily available in most department stores.

Perhaps your penchant is for rounded shapes. Though true spheres are difficult to carve (it would be easier to pour your soap into a round mold), a rounded effect can be achieved by carving. With a pencil, trace a hemisphere on both ends of your bar of soap with the help of a whiskey glass, jar lid, teacup or the end of a metal spatula. Using the outline as a guide, round these ends with a paring knife as you would peel an apple, not removing them all in one swoop, but taking off a little at a time. This will give you a bar with rounded corners but flat sides. You can try to round the flat sides by beveling the top and bottom edges. Beveling will eventually round the shape. You can refine and smooth the curve by gently wiping it with a wet paper towel.

As for other possibilities, there are many. There is actual soap-carving, the sculpting of objects and scenes out of soap. There are an estimated 300,000 soap-carving hobbyists in this country who annually compete in shows, and in all manners take the art quite to their hearts. Try it and you may find that you like soap-carving, too.

There are other things you can do. The softer soaps, after they have set in the molds a day or two, are still soft enough to be rolled into balls or modeled into whatever shapes please. They can be flattened out and cut with cookie cutters. (You can do this with the harder soaps, too, by cutting them into thin slices.)

Experiment with tools; try everything you have on hand and use whatever suits you. I find smaller utensils easier to handle than large ones, but tools are a personal matter. Professional soap-carvers who work in the soap industry and carve the bars from which dies are made have their favorite soap-carving implements—usually items found around the house. Keep an eye out for unusual tools which will give you interesting effects. There is a comblike metal utensil used to ridge icing on cake that gives odd results. Its shape is triangular, and each of its three sides is cut in a different zigzag pattern. It doesn't cost much more than a half dollar and can be found at kitchen supply stores and Eastern European spice and kitchenware shops

Working in soap—to any end and in any of its permutations—is relaxing. I have passed many a lovely evening at home with friends, about a newspaper-covered table, chatting, drinking wine, and carving soap.

DECORATIVE MOLDS

FOR FANCIFULLY shaped bars with intricate patterns, you need to use molds. If you look hard enough in your own house, you ought to be able to find a variety of intriguing receptacles that might give you interesting results. My favorite molds are the ornate plastic trays which hold rows of cookies in cellophane packages. These produce bars in all kinds of decorative shapes—one has sloping scalloped sides and a diamond pattern on top, another is heart-shaped, a third looks like a fluted log. They are very nice. Plastic sundae dishes, the kind you get from take-out ice cream shops, are another idea. I picked out a few varieties from a paper-and-party supply shop.

Plastic is perhaps the best material for a mold. You can pour your soap into ceramic, stainless steel, enamelware or glass, but you won't be able to get it out. Suction will hold the soap in place. The plastic, however, is flexible; if it can't be torn off, you can still lift the sides, which will let air in and allow you to either push or knock the soap out. Oil all molds with mineral oil to facilitate removing the soap.

When using nonflexible molds, you have the option of lining them with thin plastic wrap, though this may interfere with your shape by introducing wrinkles and round edges. You can also settle for soap "permanently" fixed in the mold; a sink-side soap ramekin that can be dabbed at with a small natural sponge is rather nice, if not exceptionally practical. Use a fancy ceramic ramekin and give it as a house gift.

You might want to use the type of mold that comes apart in two. Children's toy molds, available for all sorts of projects, can be tried. Or you can make your own plaster molds of balls, fruits, hollowed-out eggs, just about anything. Dixiecups and other paper cups, provided they are waxed, are potential molds. Think about milk and orange juice containers. Innumerable possibilities will materialize if you put your mind to it.

Also think of what you can do within the framework of your cardboard box, like pouring the soap into the box over some patterned or corrugated or furrowed material. Usually I make most of the batch in a box and the remainder in molds. If you would like to try the same, I recommend you use a box somewhat smaller than a shoe box; a gift box of some kind or a children's shoe box, or the kind that would come with ballet or bedroom slippers.

Don't use molds that are too small; dessert dishes are quite small enough, and even with those you risk the problem of too quick a drop in temperature. Quick heat loss may stop the reaction and result in a slight separation, with a thin layer of soap that is a little too caustic. Normally you could just slice this layer off. However, with a molded soap, this is hard to do without altering the shape or pattern imparted by your mold. Try washing it off. Do the best you can, and remember that your soap is not to be worried over but enjoyed.

Some Oils and Fats and the Characteristics of Their Soaps

Soap	Color	Consistency	Odor
Coconut Oil	White to yellowish	Very hard, brittle	Almost odorless
Palm Oil	White to yellowish	Very hard, brittle	Similar to oil, pleasant
Olive Oil	Yellow to drab green	Hard	Weak, oily
Peanut Oil	Light yellow	Softer than olive	Practically odorless
Soybean Oil	Light yellow to green	Hard	Practically odorless
Cottonseed Oil	Greyish to dirty yellow	Fairly soft	Similar to oil
Tallow	Yellowish	Very hard	Slightly fatty
Lard	White	Hard	Almost odorless
Shortening	Characteristics are similar to the oil the shortening is made of; color and odor are somewhat better		
Butter	Yellowish	Fairly soft	Slightly fatty

Foam	Detergent Quality	Skin Reaction
Quick big bubbles; short lasting	Good in cold sea water	Drying
Slow small bubbles	Very good	Very mild
Fair to good	Good	Very mild
Fair to good	Fairly good	Very mild
Mediocre	Mediocre	Mild
Mediocre, lasting	Good	Mild
Slow small bubbles	Good	Very mild
Quick small bubbles	Good	Very mild
Fair, small bubbles	Mediocre	Very mild